Beyond All Knowing

Beyond All Knowing

poems

Chantal Dalton

atmosphere press

© 2025 Chantal Dalton

Published by Atmosphere Press

Cover design by Ronaldo Alves

No part of this book may be reproduced without permission from the author except in brief quotations and in reviews.

Atmospherepress.com

You know who you are and why it matters

All My Time

Down what long tunnel of coincidence did we tumble to end up here?
You have all the standing; I tamp down desire.
All my remaining time is yours.

I sit down and you sit down.
Petal by petal, I toss away what shackles me,
And embrace what draws me to you;
Humor, honesty, finding a friend; finding myself
Smiling when I think of you.

And I think of you when I inhale "now" and exhale "then."
It's the now I can't know until you know.
All my remaining time is yours to spend or save;
Spend as you wish, and I'll save it all.

Breathe

You don't know how thin my heart is; how easily I lose my head,
how quickly I change my mind. Why can't I abide distance or
   silence?

You can't understand how close I need to be to you if I want to
   breathe –
and I want to breathe, to be near laughter, light and joy,
and all the gentle words we share in this blink of an eye encounter.

I remain on my path.
You remain on your path, until our destinations converge.
And if they should, my heart will expand, my head will be found,
my mind settled. I will be breathing
because distance and silence resolve
when we arrive together someplace that never was forbidden.

Beyond All Knowing

My hearing is gone. My throat is dry.
I can't catch my breath. I am silence.
Pain. Pain from a deep, empty space.
Alone, bereft, I choose to mourn
what was, what never got to be.

Beyond all knowing, I ask, why?
A ticking clock mocks my question
Offering no direction except forward – no matter what.

Behind me, I leave loss.
Ahead, I embrace all the love there is,
and all the home I can make.
A shiny answer glows in the dark:
'Let go of longing and the wish will be fulfilled.'
Wait like your life depends on it.

Moving On

You remain on my mind.
I still smile when I think of you.
Not having any standing to act, or say or be,
I float free of longing and face my blank pages alone.
I hear an electric groan on my cell to tell me
your words are there even if you are not.
I have learned to breathe, find joy, conquer distance and silence
by writing and reading and listening to my own heart.
The heart goes on; sighs cease and eyes that followed you
see only me in the mirror.
What once was longing has become real love.
I've made my own home in my own heart
with love enough for me – and more.

Be and Let Be

Your life is yours and my life is mine.
Your story is yours and my story is mine.
Our story lines merged for a moment.
Your life went left, and my life is still held
by distance and silence wrapped in uncertainty.
Loneliness is a hollow resting place
where we wait and suffer and suffer and wait.

I long to learn what it means to be enough;
to stand in the only truth I know: Love matters.
Because love matters, my hope does not falter
or pause to wonder what it is to have enough.
I am enough. I have enough to build a kingdom
in my heart that can overcome silence and distance.
Joy is a song I sing for myself.
Time is a breath unbounded by fear.
I can be, and let be; that is enough.

Nothing for It

There is nothing to be done for it.
My love is indelible. It does not wash off.
It has determination. It is fearless.
This love has its own timetable.
Love, like most good things, is happiness and wholeness.
Love is joy that rises with the sun,
sustains itself through struggles and storms;
overcomes fear and silence and distance;
a confident love that knows its name,
      and calls you by name.
This love has a destination and a home.
Nothing is lost when love prevails.
Even if one treasured thing goes away,
you are left with everything else because love prevailed.
I alone am left to tell the tale:
Love matters. The wisdom in my secret heart tells me so.
A heart no longer secret. A heart that has a home.

Leaning In

I greet you; glad to see you.
You lean in close and offer me your sweaty neck to kiss.
Of course, I kiss your neck, salty sweat and all.
Apparently, your lips are not available.
You are a key man, the center that keeps
      an enterprise stable.
I, however, am not a key woman,
so, I get the second tier of sweetness, no kiss on the cheek,
      and lips are forbidden.
You seem to refrain with intention.
I am not offended – just amused.
One can be respectful and honor age and status,
but age is just a number and status just a notion.
I am not a grandma or a mom,
so, you can decide what honor means to you.
Meanwhile, I'll keep leaning in.

Loving Joy

I am meeting love for the first time.
I've tried desire, lust, convenience, compromise,
but love is none of these. I settled.
I lost some moment in the past
that would have made me whole.
Instead, I am here –
amazed, joyful, calm; happy and sad,
confident and tentative; realistic, delusional –
navigating feelings that had no context before.
Love respects no one.
Our timelines don't match, but our spirits do.
Spirit carries me across time and space
to where all that matters is love.
Desire does not win. Impatience is hobbled.
Joy draws you into my thoughts and doubt has no name.
This love has no beginning and no end.
No hesitation, no regret.
This love has a life of its own
that neither of us can fathom or escape.
Under a scorching sun, we drink cool, cool wine.

Home

Where I live is not my home.
My clothes are there, my books, my rugs,
My mother's pictures, my husband's paintings.
There are three TVs, two smart phones,
A laptop, a tablet; kitchen appliances,
every Knick and Knack you can imagine.
Three indoor cats and two outdoor cats;
the shadowy presence of five cats we lost to death
                              in this house.
A freezer full of food; work honors on the wall,
a love seat, two recliners, two club chairs.
Everything is there but me.
My home is elsewhere in the city.
My joy is a fire pit near the urban farm you tend;
Sharing stories that make us laugh.
Joy heals absence.
If home is where the heart is, I have a home
and a reason to be there.

My Mother's Hands

I looked down surprised to see my mother's hands.
Hers were capable, strong hands; artistic, expressive.
What I see in mine is wrinkly skin, hesitance and fading purpose.

Who do I get to be now? Has everything about my life
                                        been done and said?
Scratching my pen across the page, I hope an answer
                                        will magically appear,
but misdirection is the essence of magic.
I have no neat tricks. I have no mirrors.
What I see is what I see.
Beyond memory is imagination that misdirects what I thought I
   knew.
Did I imagine her distance, her silence?
Her brooding sadness, her mysterious demeanor?
It was after I observed her in the classroom
that I realized that for her, when she came home,
I was just another one of the many children she had to watch.
I began to doubt that I had any special meaning to her.
Was I a source of curiosity or joy or love?
I was just one more kid she wanted to escape; I exhausted her.

When I was as tall as she was, I think she finally saw me as a person –
Someone who had ideas and needs, advice and opinions that had
                                              meaning for her.

Her long missing smile returned. She was breathing again.
Her divorce set her free and I began to learn who my mother
>might become.
I had status and value. We had to work together for each of us
>to have a future.
We walked together knowing a new neighborhood.

My mother's 100 years of living slipped away in silence.
Some months later, I found old photos I'd never seen.
Me as a baby, my mother glowing with joy that I was alive
>because of her.
Smiling, laughing, proud of her own baby – the one she decided to keep...
So glad I got to stay instead of being shunted out future-less.
In that one golden moment, caught on black and white film,
My mother laughed - just because.

Go On

Stay here with us. We hold you in our hearts.
More than a shadow on the doorstep
slipping away while you could only watch.
Come back to forgive yourself.
Come back to who you've always been:
Love made flesh; the "overcomer," a man of
                             courageous kindness
who soaks up loss and sheds fear;
who faces a final silence unable to let go.
The fissures love has not yet healed will heal;
love will prevail.

We must let go to live as we lived before –
Unapologetic for being here, encouraged by
                             every living thing
that feels this life as legacy.
You have a fear that lurks in darkness
threatening to swallow the future.
Then is no longer here; now aches to recover.
Tomorrow has its own defining moment.
You can exhale now. You can cry along with us.
Take another deep breath and let it go -
         again and again and again,
and go on.

Unlimited

No expiration date on the love I share.
Always fresh, valid, timeless and unlimited.
My love stays the course, conquers marathons
                       and eliminates redundancies.
Even once can be enough for a lifetime.
No need to count the time.
You have all my remaining time.
No distance, no silence. Floating.
Somewhere between hello and goodbye – love, so much love.
Hello just got started.

Shadow

Seeing the photos you sent made me smile,
showing me places I never expected to visit or see.
A mysterious mansion far off on the horizon.
A pond standing on its own, serene, though apart
from a manmade stone shack and a manmade wall,
all framed by a tree stretching out leafless arms
                      pleading to a cloudy sky.
Bales of hay stacked and ready for their fate.
And you, a shadow in your own picture,
your presence altering the perspective.
Even a shadow can conquer distance and time.
You are your own time continuum and make it possible
        for me to conquer space.
How short the distance between where I am and where you are:
the reflection of a shadow shrinks the gap.

Big Easy

I close my eyes and see your face. I hear you call my name.
By some digital process I do not understand, you appear on my
   phone.
I am on the Natchez. You are home in the backyard chopping wood.
I am thrilled to see you, to know that I am somewhere,
and you are somewhere else at the same time talking to me:
a "disembodied voice" embodied.

To see you and hear your voice without a Zoom connection -
just you and me talking, you, alone, and everyone else around me
unaware that I hold your face in my hand smiling up at me
from my phone.
You said you saw joy in my face,
not realizing that it was not just the ride on a steamboat
in the harbor
that made me smile, but sharing this moment with you
there on the farm and me here in the city you love.
New Orleans, Big Easy bringing us together, defying distance.
My here, is there with you. Your there, is here with me. Time collapses
as together we hear the steamboat whistle and the jazz band
tuning up in the background for the second set.
I reach out to you not knowing how to make the connection work.
You make it work. That is the joy you see:
my face seeing your face before me on my phone.
Joy overjoyed.

The Wood Pile

What waits at the bottom of the wood pile?
More wood. The loamy earth underneath the wood.
Insects scurrying around frantic, exposed.
The sweat it took to chop that wood into logs for the fire.
The strength it took to stick to the task.
Find leaves blackened by the pressure of logs choking out the sun;
slick and soggy from rainwater seeping underneath
that pile of wood that never seems to change.

I know we've burned many, many logs,
all chopped by you by hand -
wearing safety goggles, work gloves and a wool cap,
a ragged scarf at your neck.
You swing the axe as an extension of your arm.
Here at the farm, I am sitting at a backyard table,
notebook open, pen poised to write.
Squinting at the sun, I covertly watch you work,
wondering what it's like to swing an axe, to split a log,
toss it on the pile and swing the axe again.
With focus and facility, you create the chunks
of murdered trees we burn for warmth when the sallow sun
makes us shiver.
As the words I scratch across the page stretch my thoughts in ink,
the wood pile turns your sweat into flame.

An Afternoon at the Farm

Your lips kiss my cheek
My knees nearly go weak.
But happily, they hold
Since titanium doesn't fold.

I am getting stronger.
My bladder holds longer.
The longer I wait,
My patience is great.

I try not to shiver,
But you, being a giver,
Present me your jacket.
I feel sorry you lack it.

The fire runs so wild,
My fear is not mild.
You did what you could
By adding more wood.

If one hug is groovy,
Then surely you move me
Since you hug me twice;
Such joy in my life.

The afternoon is survivable.
    The future is laudable.
    When you finish your all,
    Please give me a call.
If it's week after next,
Just send me a text.

Never Goodbye

I never want to say goodbye, farewell or 'See you later.'
Later seems an endless break in the conversation we have started.
You have an album of word pictures of my life.
I have several snapshots of yours.
Do you tell other people the things you've told to me?
Are my secrets scattered about your house,
while I save yours at the edge of my mind?
Are my poems your haven and refuge?
Or just writing that disappears on a frosty window under a
    ruthless sun?
Tell me more or tell me not one other thing.
If unsatisfied, my Pisces mind will create a past for you,
a past I never knew but can imagine.
Drinking too much in the Big Easy, hurting too much to break
    free.
Not another word exchanged. No acknowledgment or redress.
Love squandered and dishonored,
your twenties went up in smoke and drowned in tequila shots.
When you could breathe again, as some often do,
you disappeared and slept a while. Yesterday lost its grip.
Waking up in Washington, you found the truth shaky and pale.
There was a crack in everything, but that was how the light got in.
That light showed you the way out.
Freedom is at once all there is and nothing at all.
Give a quick glance over your shoulder, say goodbye to all that,
and step into the spotlight.

Disavowed

You say if time, life and the world had lined up differently,
we might have been some kind of couple – true screamers.
You'd be smart enough not to live with me,
and I'd be wise enough not to let you.
Can't imagine getting mad at you (I do my own dishes)
or you getting mad at me (you come and go as you please).
Together or apart, then (in a dream) and now in the yard
behind your house, I declare you wrong to think
we would have disagreed or fought or thrown
books or cups at each other; that just isn't me.
But suppose that *is* you?
I wouldn't be sitting here asking you to add a log to the fire,
smiling as you demonstrate how scattered and shaggy
a pair we would have been.
Good thing I didn't meet you or know you sooner.
I wouldn't be sitting here longing to hear you whisper instead of
    shout –
Longing to make you sigh.
I'm leaving you to your own devices,
Just as I said I would;
Be and let be
without me.

Chopping Block

On the chopping block you made for me,
I am chopping vegetables into smaller pieces
to make stir fry later.
I sing silly love songs while chopping celery into tiny bits
and broccoli into little crowns;
I slice big white mushrooms in half
and then in half again and add one more.
Pepper and onion round off the chopping task
for the morning; my medley ends with
'The very thought of you.'
I am bewitched, bothered and bewildered
When I see your face before me.
My heart stood still and I'll be seeing you
In my life, because if ever I would leave you,
it wouldn't be in springtime.
With every sigh I become more mad about you.
We looked at each other in the same way then.
I can't remember where or when, but I'll get by
as long as I have you until it's time for me to go.
The song has ended, but the melody lingers on.

Except for You

I am not "in love" with you.
There'll be no conclusion
To the illusion
That there is a future
In this non-union.
Your world is yours
And my world is mine.

I leave behind almost
All that is you,
And more firmly embrace
All that is me.

My pen remembers
A closed door, a closed heart;
An end to revelry.
Except for you,
There'd be no poetry,
No sky, no sea.
I introduced me to myself again.
I have a destination
And a home within.
You opened the door and said,
"Begin."

Answers

Why do I feel I need answers
to all the questions I ask you in my poems?
Your business is yours, and my business is mine.
And yet, a niggling doubt seeps into my curiosity.
Patience has never been my strong suit.
I wait for more, but there is no more to be had.
All that makes me whole remains, was never missing.
My understanding and courage expand.
Not someday, but one day, one day after another,
tells me there is no need to know:
Nothing in shadow, nothing to seek.
We are where we are supposed to be.
A love that is fundamental links us
for however long it takes to see and believe.

Hammock

We talked about skydiving, spearfishing, and kayaking –
none of which I've ever done, but if I were brave enough,
I'd aspire to try.
Instead, I am facing my fear of hammocks (yes, hammocks).
Fear of falling out of one, specifically.
Like Goldilocks, the first one I tried was too small:
We all know why that's true!
Usually off kilter, I can't make my body lay straight.
It is always hard for me to center myself. It always has been.
You helped me feel how to lay straight.
I finally found my center.
The second hammock, the one you usually use,
is made of sterner stuff (parachute silk),
so, I was more confident.
My still oversized behind now had more room to spread out.
You helped me into that swinging marvel,
confirmed that I was okay,
and you disappeared for a while.
Dreaming and drifting, staring at clouds, so did I.

At the Farm 2

I walk with a little assistance.
Often, someone kindly offers their arm.
If not, my cane (which I consider a prop)
                        is what I lean on.
The Farm is my favorite hideout
when things are lonely, sad or dull.
The walking path was always a challenge,
but I persevered since I wanted to pick
some herbs and pat the kale.
I returned later that week and that path
                        had been improved.
I could walk easily with just a wobble or two.
When I want to get somewhere worthwhile,
I try to find level ground -
a way to steady myself, keep my balance,
                        and persist.
Seeing you is always worthwhile since
you are my level ground,
and don't mind my wobble or two.

Proof

Silence can be weightless.
Silence can carry us across time
until it feels safe to speak again.
Words forced into silence press us down
until breath is strangled speechless.
What we don't say weighs on us the most.
What does it take to lift that weight?
Together we bear the silence better than alone.
Your hand in mine is weightless.
A deep breath steadies my heart.
There is no 'let be.' I already am.
I crack the silence, and you break it.
I insist that you are the sweetest man I know.
You kiss the hand that holds yours and prove it.

Snow Bird

Some of us have all the life we were meant to have.
The rest of us - not so much.
Waiting for it all to become clear,
I'm watching football, snacking, feeding the cats,
folding clothes, cooking as little as possible
and avoiding take-out (too oily).
The chill in the air reminds me
that summer has flown.
I pull out wool scarves and hats,
gloves and the unworn snow boots from last year.
You keep wishing for snow. You fly somewhere
to find some. I stay warm.
Back with snow glow and a lighter spirit,
you are more yourself, and I remain me,
the one who notices things, watches the sky,
hears birds retreating at dusk.
I swish through dried leaves in the yard.
Glad to see you again, I heat up lentil soup
and sit down ready to hear your stories.
You already know mine.

Take Leave

I pull time's stretch band off and put it on the bedside table.
With time suspended, I step out into the night and disappear.
There is no daystar in the darkness.
Lost under night stars, I close my eyes.
With my heart's eye, I see your face.
Fearless, I embrace the city's silence.
The silence unfolds a space for me to sing.
Is it the silence or the song that keeps me awake?
The song overcomes the silence with the stroke of a pen.
Head music, heart music,
I make up the lyrics as I go along.
I trace a path that I have walked before.
When we give ourselves away,
joy is almost too much to bear.
My destination bends toward home.
Safe at home, we can sit down together
and take leave of each other.
Wait for the daystar to appear.
It is not far. It won't be long.
No need to wonder what the end will be.

About Atmosphere Press

Founded in 2015, Atmosphere Press was built on the principles of Honesty, Transparency, Professionalism, Kindness, and Making Your Book Awesome. As an ethical and author-friendly hybrid press, we stay true to that founding mission today.

If you're a reader, enter our giveaway for a free book here:

SCAN TO ENTER
BOOK GIVEAWAY

If you're a writer, submit your manuscript for consideration here:

SCAN TO SUBMIT
MANUSCRIPT

And always feel free to visit Atmosphere Press and our authors online at atmospherepress.com. See you there soon!

About the Author

CHANTAL DALTON is a "recovering" poet. She has returned to writing poetry after a long hiatus and is delighted to re-discover her poetic voice. Ms. Dalton is a graduate of Bates College (BA) and has a master's degree in American Literature from Northwestern University. In addition, she has a Master's of Science Degree in National Security Strategy from the National Defense University, National War College, Fort McNair, Washington, DC.

She taught English at Rutgers, the State University of New Jersey, serving at both the Queen's College, New Brunswick, and Livingston College campuses.

Ms. Dalton's primary career was as a Foreign Service Officer, first for the United States Information Agency and later with the Department of State after the Agency merger.

Chantal Dalton lives in Washington, DC with her husband and three crazy rescue cats who they adore. This is Ms. Dalton's first published poetry collection.

www.ingramcontent.com/pod-product-compliance
Lightning Source LLC
LaVergne TN
LVHW041643070526
838199LV00053B/3524